MAY - - 2010

TRANSCENDING RACE IN AMERICA
BIOGRAPHIES OF BIRACIAL ACHIEVERS

Halle Berry

Beyoncé

David Blaine

Mariah Carey

Frederick Douglass

W. E. B. Du Bois

Salma Hayek

Derek Jeter

Alicia Keys

Soledad O'Brien

Rosa Parks

Prince

Booker T. Washington

DEREK JETER

All-Star Major League Baseball Player

Chuck Bednar

Mason Crest Publishers

Produced by 21st Century Publishing and Communications, Inc.

MASON CREST PUBLISHERS INC.
370 Reed Road
Broomall, Pennsylvania 19008
(866) MCP-BOOK (toll free)
www.masoncrest.com

Printed in the United States of America.

First Printing

9 8 7 6 5 4 3 2 1

Library of Congress Cataloging-in-Publication Data

Bednar, Chuck, 1976–
    Derek Jeter : all-star major league baseball player / Chuck Bednar.
        p. cm. — (Transcending race in America : biographies of biracial achievers)
    Includes bibliographical references and index.
    ISBN 978-1-4222-1610-1 (hardback : alk. paper) — ISBN 978-1-4222-1624-8 (pbk. : alk. paper)
    1. Jeter, Derek, 1974–   —Juvenile literature. 2. Baseball players—United States—
Biography—Juvenile literature. I. Title.
GV865.J48B43 2010
796.357092—dc22
[B]   2009022043

Publisher's notes:
All quotations in this book come from original sources, and contain the spelling and grammatical inconsistencies of the original text.

The Web sites mentioned in this book were active at the time of publication. The publisher is not responsible for Web sites that have changed their addresses or discontinued operation since the date of publication. The publisher will review and update the Web site addresses each time the book is reprinted.

Table of Contents

" I HAVE BROTHERS, SISTERS, NIECES,
NEPHEWS, UNCLES, AND COUSINS,
OF EVERY RACE AND EVERY HUE,
SCATTERED ACROSS THREE CONTINENTS,
AND FOR AS LONG AS I LIVE,
I WILL NEVER FORGET THAT
IN NO OTHER COUNTRY ON EARTH
IS MY STORY EVEN POSSIBLE. "

" WE MAY HAVE DIFFERENT STORIES,
BUT WE HOLD COMMON HOPES. . . .
WE MAY NOT LOOK THE SAME
AND WE MAY NOT HAVE
COME FROM THE SAME PLACE,
BUT WE ALL WANT TO MOVE
IN THE SAME DIRECTION —
TOWARDS A BETTER FUTURE . . . "

— BARACK OBAMA, 44TH PRESIDENT
OF THE UNITED STATES OF AMERICA

1

HITTING MILESTONES

BABE RUTH, LOU GEHRIG, AND DEREK JETER are three New York Yankees greats who will forever be linked by the events of September 2008. During that month, Derek set his sights on records set by both Baseball Hall of Famers, and prepared to take his place alongside them in the pages of franchise history.

Since making his Major League Baseball debut in 1995, Derek had already proven his baseball **prowess** on several occasions. He was a nine-time All-Star, a four-time World Series champion, and the recipient of several other awards and honors. His feats during the final month of the 2008 season would only add to his legacy as one of the best ballplayers of his era.

PASSING THE BABE

Derek had spent much of the 2008 season setting hitting **milestones**. In June 2008, he passed Mickey Mantle and moved

Derek Jeter hits a home run to tie Lou Gehrig's record for the most career hits at Yankee Stadium on September 14, 2008. That season Derek reached several other hitting milestones, including third-youngest player to get 2,500 career hits, and he passed both Mickey Mantle's and Babe Ruth's records of hits for the Yankees.

into third place on the Yankees' list of all-time hits leaders. He followed that up with his 2,500th career hit in an August 22 game against the Baltimore Orioles, becoming the third-youngest player in baseball history at the time to do so. After that game, a mere 18 hits separated Derek and the second place Ruth.

By September 7, just two hits separated the Yankee greats. On that day, in a game against the Seattle Mariners, Derek had a base hit and a home run to tie the Babe. The following day, he went hitless against the Anaheim Angels, but on September 9, Derek had his date with destiny. In the first inning, he hit a single to left field off Anaheim pitcher Ervin Santana to take sole possession of second place. New York won the game and afterwards, Derek reflected on his accomplishment while speaking to MLB.com.

In 2008, Derek was chasing hitting records held by Lou Gehrig (left) and Babe Ruth. On September 9, Derek slugged a base hit and home run to break Babe Ruth's record, moving into second place on the list of all-time Yankees hit leaders.

> **"**It's kind of hard to believe. I don't know how else I can say it. If you play long enough, and you're consistent enough, maybe some good things happen. I guess I've been fortunate. Anytime you're mentioned in the same sentence with players like that, it feels good.**"**

Baseball Legends: Babe Ruth and Lou Gehrig

There have been many great New York Yankee baseball players throughout the years, but Babe Ruth and Lou Gehrig were two of the finest. George Herman Ruth was born in 1895 and was nicknamed the "Babe" and the "Sultan of Swat." During his career, Babe Ruth was a three-time All-Star, a seven-time World Series champion, and the 1923 American League MVP. He also hit 714 career home runs and was elected to the Baseball Hall of Fame in 1936.

Lou Gehrig, born in 1903, was called the "Iron Horse" because of his durability. He played 2,130 consecutive games, a long-standing record broken in 1995, and won two American League MVP awards during his career. The seven-time All-Star and six-time World Series champion was eventually forced out of the game due to ALS, a degenerative neurological disease. Gehrig was inducted into the Hall of Fame in 1939. Both players have had their respective numbers retired by the Yankees.

His performance against the Angels that night gave him 2,520 career hits, putting him roughly 200 hits behind the all-time Yankees leader in that statistical category, Lou Gehrig. Obviously, with the 2008 season winding down, that milestone would have to wait. However, Derek did have another one of the Iron Horse's records in his sights.

CHASING THE IRON HORSE

On September 14, the Yankees were in the middle of their final home stand at the original Yankee Stadium. No other player in team history had more hits at the **venerable** ballpark than Gehrig's 1,269, but as he and his teammates took the field against the Tampa Bay Rays, Derek was only a mere three hits back in second place.

In the first inning, he reached on a bunt single. He followed that with a second inning double, closing the difference to a single hit. In the fifth inning, Derek again stepped up to the plate. Facing David Price, a rookie making his Major League Baseball debut, Derek worked the count to 2-2 before lifting a pitch over the wall in right-center field. Not only did he tie Gehrig's record, but he did it in style, with a solo home run.

The following evening, against the Chicago White Sox, Derek went hitless in four at-bats as the eager crowd looked on, hoping to see him make history. The 34-year-old shortstop later jokingly blamed his performance on the flash bulbs from all the fans hoping to catch the historic moment. It was impossible to tell whether he was actually feeling the pressure or not, thanks to his trademark calm and poised demeanor, but the clock was ticking. He had just six more games to break the Yankee Stadium hits record, or else the opportunity would be lost forever.

Yankee Stadium

The original Yankee Stadium was built in 1923 in the Bronx area of New York City. It was home of the Yankees for 50 years following its opening, and after renovations, once again hosted the team's games from 1976 through 2008. It is also known as "The House that Ruth Built" in honor of the legendary Babe Ruth, and as of the start of the 2009 season, had hosted more World Series games than any other baseball venue. The final game at old Yankee Stadium was held on September 21, 2008, as the Yankees beat the Baltimore Orioles, 7-3.

AN UNBREAKABLE RECORD

On September 16, the Yankees again took the home field to face Chicago. Derek's quest for the stadium hits record was once again the primary focus of the more than 52,000 fans on hand for the game. They didn't have to wait long to see history made. During his first at-bat, Derek hit a ball toward third base that got through the legs of Chicago's Juan Uribe. Derek reached first base safely as the crowd waited, wondering if it would be ruled a hit or an error.

Derek runs the bases after hitting a home run over the right-field wall to tie Lou Gehrig's Yankee Stadium hitting record. After that, the pressure mounted because Derek only had six more games to break the stadium record before the ballpark would be closed forever.

Derek proudly waves to the crowd after his first-inning single against the Chicago White Sox on September 16, 2008. The hit (his 1,270th at Yankee stadium) swept him past Lou Gehrig's record. Derek was thrilled to be part of baseball history, with a record that could never be broken.

After what seemed like an endless delay, the ground ball was indeed ruled a hit, and the crowd roared their approval. Derek had done it. He had moved past Gehrig, and even went on to add another hit that evening for good measure. He had set an unbreakable record—one that would remain in the books forever once Yankee Stadium closed at season's end. Afterward, he described his feelings to MLB.com's Samantha Newman:

> **"[My parents] were saying, 'You need to sit back and try to enjoy it while it's happening,' because I'm always thinking about how we can win and things like that. But this is pretty special. I'd be lying if I said it wasn't. . . . There's so much history at Yankee Stadium, and just to be a part of it is something special."**

Derek Jeter is something special as well. Throughout his entire career, he has been the cornerstone of some truly great teams. He has won numerous awards for his on-field play and created numerous memorable moments for baseball fans in the **Big Apple**. He has become a celebrity off the field as well, appearing on TV shows, using his fame for charitable causes, and even catching the eye of some of the loveliest ladies in show business. Whether it is on the baseball diamond or in other aspects of life, Derek Jeter shows the world what it means to be an achiever.

2

❦

FAMILY AND BASEBALL

DEREK SANDERSON JETER WAS BORN IN Pequannock, New Jersey, on June 26, 1974. His father Charles was an African-American psychologist, and his mother was an accountant of Irish and German descent. Derek's later successes in life and in baseball are largely due to his family, and the lessons he learned as a child.

His father, Dr. Charles Jeter, was raised by his mother in a single-parent home in Alabama. Meanwhile, Derek's mother, Dorothy, was one of 14 daughters of a church custodian, Sonny Connors, and his wife Dorothy. When Derek was four years old, the Jeter family moved to Kalamazoo, Michigan, so that his father could earn his Ph.D. in psychology from Western Michigan University.

Derek and his sister Sharlee spent most of their childhood in Kalamazoo, but they often returned to New Jersey to visit their

Derek was involved in sports at an early age. His father loved baseball, so Derek and his sister followed in those footsteps. The family always rooted for the Yankees, and once Derek promised his father he would someday play in the Detroit ballpark where they had seen the Yankees play.

grandparents. They learned many lessons from their family, but the most important was the value of hard work. Both Derek's mother, Dorothy, and his grandfather, Sonny, worked long hours to support the family but still found the time to volunteer their time to help out people in need.

Other Multiracial Athletes

Derek Jeter is one of many amazing athletes, past and present, to have a multiracial family background. Golfing great Tiger Woods, a winner of 14 major golf championships, is of mixed Chinese, Thai, African-American, Native-American, and Dutch ancestry. One of the greatest athletes of all time, Jim Thorpe, was part Native American, part French, and part Irish.

Furthermore, Pro Football Hall of Famer Franco Harris, a nine-time Pro Bowler and a four-time Super Bowl Champion, has an African-American father and an Italian mother. In basketball, 2007 NBA Finals MVP Tony Parker has an African-American father and a Dutch mother. Even former NCAA football player, professional wrestler, and actor Dwayne "The Rock" Johnson is part Black Canadian and part Samoan.

LIKE FATHER, LIKE SON

Athletic ability ran in the Jeter family. Charles played baseball in his youth and was a shortstop at Fisk University at Tennessee. Derek and Sharlee both followed in his footsteps. Sharlee played softball, while Derek became involved first in Little League and then in high school baseball. As he told the Sports Illustrated Web site,

> **"I always idolized my dad, so I loved baseball too. . . . I always rooted for the Yankees. . . . Once or twice a year, when the Yankees came to Detroit, we would make the two-and-a-half-hour drive to Tiger Stadium. On one of those trips, my father recalls, I promised him that I would play in that ballpark someday."**

Growing up, Derek was inspired by Yankee great Dave Winfield, and was intensely competitive—but not always in a good way. Once, following a loss in a Little League game, Derek refused to shake hands with the opposing players. His **irate** father told Derek that he needed to learn how to play tennis because he "obviously [didn't] know how to play a team sport."

Through it all, though, Derek learned and grew. He blossomed into a star on the diamond, and in 1992, he won High School Player of the Year honors from the American Baseball Coaches Association, *USA Today*, and Gatorade. As luck would have it, he was drafted by his beloved New York Yankees sixth overall in

One of Derek's early idols was Hall of Famer and Yankee great Dave Winfield. Like Winfield, Derek had a competitive drive. But when he didn't display good sportsmanship as well, his father grew angry and insisted Derek show more team spirit.

In his first year as a minor leaguer, Derek struggled with his play and with being away from home. Both his father and his coach continued to encourage him, and within a couple of years, three magazines had named him the 1994 Minor League Player of the Year.

the Major League Baseball draft that year. He was the first high school player taken that year, and despite a brief stint as a student at the University of Michigan, he was set to become a professional baseball player.

MINOR LEAGUE UPS AND DOWNS

Derek's minor league baseball career didn't exactly get off to a great start. In his first year, he struggled in both Tampa and Greensboro, North Carolina. He committed a whopping 56 errors that year, and as he told *Sports Illustrated*, he often turned to his parents for advice.

> **"I was homesick for Kalamazoo every day. I was struggling for the first time—I hit .210 that summer—and being away from my family and everything familiar to me was tough. I ran up $300-a-month phone bills, calling home after almost every game."**

With reassuring comments from his father and the assistance of Coach Brian Butterfield, Derek was able to turn his game around. In 1993, he hit .295 and drove in 71 runs with Greensboro. He was also second in the South Atlantic League with 11 triples and third with 152 hits. South Atlantic League managers named him the Most Outstanding Major League Prospect, while *Baseball America* dubbed Derek the Best Defensive Shortstop and the Most Exciting Player in the league.

The following year, Derek spent time with teams in Tampa and Albany, New York, before being called up to the Triple-A Columbus Clippers, one step away from the big leagues. He hit a combined .344 with the three teams, adding 68 RBIs, 5 home runs, and 50 stolen bases. Derek was named the 1994 Minor League Player of the Year by *Baseball America*, *The Sporting News*, and *Baseball Weekly*. Through hard work, Derek had **persevered** and overcome his early struggles. Now he clearly was on the way to being called up to the big leagues.

SHORTSTOP, STAR PLAYER, AND SOCIALITE

DEREK MADE HIS MAJOR LEAGUE BASEBALL debut on May 29, 1995, replacing the injured Tony Fernandez at shortstop against the Seattle Mariners. Starting alongside Don Mattingly and Wade Boggs, in his first major league game Derek went hitless in five at-bats. It was an **inauspicious** debut, but the next day he did manage to record his first big league hit.

Derek only played in 15 games in 1995, not enough to officially qualify as a rookie. The following season, he was named an opening day starter, becoming the first Yankee rookie to start at shortstop in 34 years. He soon proved worthy of the honor, playing in 157 games and hitting .314 with 10 home runs and 78 RBIs (runs batted in) during the regular season. Derek's excellent play continued in the postseason. He hit .361 in the playoffs as the Yankees won the 1996 World Series.

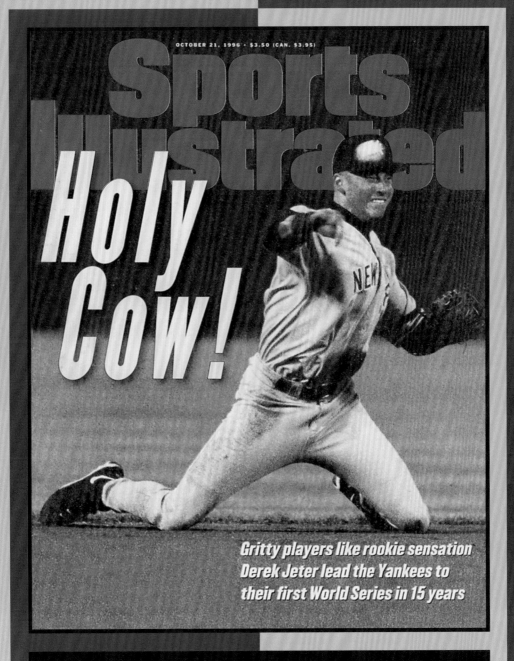

OCTOBER 21, 1996 · $3.50 (CAN. $3.95)

Sports Illustrated

Holy Cow!

Gritty players like rookie sensation Derek Jeter lead the Yankees to their first World Series in 15 years

In his first official season with the Yankees, Derek was the first rookie to start at shortstop in 34 years. His team went on to win the 1996 World Series, and Derek was named American League Rookie of the Year.

ESTABLISHING HIS PRESENCE

As if becoming a World Series champion in his first full year in the Major Leagues wasn't enough, Derek was also named the American League Rookie of the Year. Not only that, but he became just the fifth player to win it **unanimously**. It was a well-deserved honor, as New York manager Joe Torre told Jack Curry of *The New York Times* on November 5, 1996:

"I don't think we had one guy, player-wise, who was more valuable than him. . . . His hitting blew me out of the tub. I never expected anything like that."

The New York Yankees

No other professional baseball team in North American has won as many titles as the New York Yankees. Through December 2008, the franchise had won 26 World Series titles and 39 American League pennants. Also, some of the best baseball players ever have donned the team's trademark pinstripe uniforms, including Hall of Famers Babe Ruth, Lou Gehrig, Mickey Mantle, Joe DiMaggio, Yogi Berra, Whitey Ford, and Reggie Jackson.

Originally founded in Baltimore, the team was purchased by Frank Farrell and Bill Devery and moved to the Big Apple in 1903. At first, the team was known as the Highlanders but became the Yankees in 1913. They called the Polo Grounds home until 1923, when Yankee Stadium opened and became their primary field for the next several decades. The team is known by many nicknames, including "The Yanks" and the "Bronx Bombers."

That off-season, Derek and his family started the Turn 2 Foundation, an organization established to help keep kids away from drugs and alcohol and direct them toward healthier lifestyles. In 1997, he earned his first MVP votes, playing in 159 games and tallying 190 hits. Unfortunately, the Yankees lost in the first round and were unable to repeat as champions. It was a disappointing end to the season for the storied baseball franchise.

Once again, Derek made off-season news. First, he and teammate Bernie Williams appeared on the TV show *Seinfeld*. Later, after he was spotted on the set of a Mariah Carey music video, it

The Yankees have won more American League and World Series championships than any other team. Although they didn't make it to the World Series in 1997, Derek began his winning momentum that year and received his first-ever votes for Most Valuable Player.

was revealed that the singer and the Yankee shortstop were dating. They were together throughout spring training and much of the season before calling it quits in June, citing media pressure as the cause for their breakup.

Derek had an awesome year in 1998. Off the field, he won endorsement deals and was linked with glamorous songstress Mariah Carey. During the season he led the league in runs scored, was voted into the All-Star Game, and helped the Yankees win their second World Series championship in three years.

A SEASON FOR THE AGES

With or without Mariah in his life, Derek enjoyed an exceptional 1998 season, as did the New York Yankees as a team. That year, he led the American League with 127 runs scored, had more than 200 hits for the first time in his career, and was voted into his first-ever All-Star Game. More importantly, however, he helped the team rebound from the disappointment of 1997 in a big way—the Yankees won a franchise record 114 games in 1998.

With so many regular season victories under their belts, the 1998 Yankees had a real claim at being one of the best teams ever. To do so, however, Derek and his teammates knew they would have to continue their winning ways in the playoffs. They did just that, sweeping the Texas Rangers in the American League Division Series (ALDS), beating the Cleveland Indians in six games, and then taking four straight from San Diego Padres to claim their second World Series title in three years. Were they the best ever? As Torre told the Associated Press,

> **"I don't know if we have the best team of all time, but I do know that we have the best record. . . . It's the best club I've ever been around."**

Derek, meanwhile, had set an American League record for most runs scored by a shortstop during the first three years of his career (352). He had also finished third in the MVP voting and continued to enjoy success off the field as well. During the season, he had become the spokesman for Skippy brand peanut butter, becoming the first athlete ever to do commercials for the product. He also appeared on the cover of *GQ* magazine, and in early 1999 he signed on to become a spokesman for Nike.

REACHING THE NEXT LEVEL

Considering all that he had already accomplished, it may be hard to believe that Derek's baseball career would soon reach even greater heights. The truth was, however, that 1999 would be his finest season to date. He set career highs with a .349 batting average, a .438 on-base percentage, a .552 slugging percentage, 24 home runs, 102 RBIs, 9 triples, and 91 walks. Derek also made the All-Star Game for the second straight year.

Boosted largely by Derek's outstanding performance, the Yankees won 98 games and claimed the AL East division title. New York swept the Rangers once again in the first round. Next, they upended the rival Boston Red Sox in five games to win the AL pennant and return to the World Series. There, they made short work of the Atlanta Braves, sweeping their National League

Derek steals a base during the first game of the 1999 World Series against the Atlanta Braves. The 1999 season saw Derek's stats reach new highs, with a batting average of .349, 24 home runs, and 102 RBIs. He played in the All-Star Game for the second straight year and was a key player in the Yankees' World Series victory.

opponent to repeat as baseball champions. After the decisive fourth game, Braves pitcher John Smoltz told reporters what everyone watching already knew:

> **"The best team won. The Yankees are head and shoulders above most when it comes to this time of the year. We lost to the best team, simply put. . . . The Yankees are a model of how to win."**

Derek hit .375 in the postseason and had clearly emerged as a rising star. By this time, the Yankee shortstop even had his own brand of breakfast cereal. Eager to keep him in New York, team ownership attempted to work out a long-term deal with him. Negotiations broke down, however, and Derek wound up signing a one-year deal for $10 million. He proved his worth by winning the All-Star Game MVP award, posting his third straight 200-hit season, and leading the Yankees back into the World Series.

TOAST OF THE TOWN

Opposing the Yankees were the New York Mets, making the 2000 World Series the first "Subway Series" since 1956. The first game was a real dogfight, with the Yankees outlasting the Mets 4-3 in the longest game in World Series history. In game two, the Yankees built up a 6-0 lead before the Mets came back, scoring five times in the ninth inning but falling one run short in the end.

The National League club won the third game, but the next two belonged to the Yankees, as Derek hit one home run in each game. The American Leaguers from New York had won their third straight World Series championship, and this time, Derek won MVP honors as he hit .409, scored six runs, and drove in two others en route to the title. As one CNNSI.com writer observed after the game, he was definitely a worthy recipient of that award.

> **"Jeter has become the Yankees' central character, a clutch performer with a Mona Lisa smile who seems to get better when the games become more**

important. . . . He's played just five major league seasons and already has four World Series rings . . . and his best years are still ahead.**"**

The Subway Series

The term "Subway Series" is used to describe a group of baseball games played between two different New York–based franchises. Traditionally, the word has been used to describe World Series matchups, though with the invention of interleague play in 1997, it can apply to regular season games as well. The 2000 Subway Series featured the Yankees against the Mets. Prior to their moves to the West Coast, however, the Brooklyn Dodgers and the New York Giants were also part of many Subway Series.

In 1921 and 1922, the Giants and Yankees met in back-to-back World Series that were held at a single ballpark, as both teams played home games at the Polo Grounds. From 1923 through 1953, the Yankees played in nine different New York–only World Series, beating either the Giants or Dodgers in all of them. Prior to 2000, the last Subway Series had been held in 1956, with the Yankees beating Brooklyn in seven games. The 2000 World Series marked the first time the Mets had participated in a playoff-based Subway Series.

Derek had definitely become the toast of the town. He had become the first player in baseball history to win the All-Star Game and World Series MVP awards in the same year, all while dating former Miss Universe Lara Dutta. In February 2001, he was rewarded with a 10-year, $189 million deal. It would turn out to be a wise investment, as Derek once again earned a trip to the All-Star Game and became the first Yankee since Yogi Berra to hit a home run during the "Mid-Summer Classic."

PLAYOFFS AND PERSPECTIVE

The Yankees ran away with the American League East that year, and were preparing for the playoffs when tragedy struck. On September 11, 2001, terrorists crashed two planes into the World Trade Center in New York, killing more than 2,000 people. Baseball halted the season in the wake of the horrific events of that day, allowing Derek and his teammates to travel to what

Derek vaulted into celebrity status in 2000. Once again he was offered commercial endorsements and had a 200-hit season. If that weren't enough, he was the first player to win both World Series and All-Star Game MVP awards in the same year.

Derek forces Oakland A's Eric Chavez out at second base then completes the double play with a throw to first in the second inning of game four of the American League Division Series in Oakland in 2001. Derek's amazing play helped the Yankees stay in the playoffs, but they later lost the World Series.

became known as "Ground Zero" and assist local police and fire-fighters with the rescue efforts. He later discussed the experience with MLB.com.

"I think it really puts things in perspective for a lot of people. . . . It was a rough time, but then when we came back, we understood what our role was. I think

people appreciated watching us during that time because it gave them something that they could cheer for at least maybe three hours a day."

Once play did resume, Derek and the Yankees returned to the task of trying to win another World Series championship. New York faced the Athletics in the ALDS, and during Game 3 of the series, Derek made one of the best plays in baseball history— tracking down an errant throw from the outfield and flipping the ball to catcher Jorge Posada in time to force Oakland's Jason Giambi out at the plate. Derek also broke Pete Rose's all-time playoff hitting record, but unfortunately the Yankees fell to the Arizona Diamondbacks in the World Series.

MOVING ON

In December 2001, Derek hosted the popular *Saturday Night Live* television show. On April 1, 2002, he hit his 100th career home run against the Baltimore Orioles. He finished that season with 191 hits and 32 stolen bases, both third among American League players. He also became just the fourth player in Major League Baseball history to score at least 100 runs in each of his first four seasons.

New York again won the AL East in 2002. This time, however, they failed to even reach the World Series, losing to the Anaheim Angels in the first round of the playoffs. Despite the fact that he hit .500 in the series, Derek was disappointed with the outcome and determined to do whatever he could to elevate the team back to its former glory. It was for that attitude that the Yankee shortstop was about to earn a very special honor.

TEAM CAPTAIN

IT WAS BUSINESS AS USUAL FOR DEREK following the end of the 2002 season. After a long **hiatus** from the dating scene, he was spotted Christmas shopping with actress Jordana Brewster. By the time spring training rolled around, however, the two were no longer an item, and Derek's focus returned to his first love, baseball.

The 2003 season got off to a rough start, as a shoulder injury in a game against the Toronto Blue Jays caused him to miss six weeks in April and May. Playing largely without him, New York managed just a 32-23 record through the end of May. Those struggles emphasized exactly how important Derek was to the team. So on June 3, Derek Jeter was named the 11th team captain in New York Yankees history, and the first since Don Mattingly retired in 1995. As owner George Steinbrenner told *The New York Times*,

Derek became the Yankees' 11th team captain in 2003. Team owner George Steinbrenner was full of admiration for Derek's leadership ability. The Yankees agreed and won 101 games that season, 6 games ahead of their archrivals, the Boston Red Sox.

"My gut tells me this would be a good time for Derek Jeter to assume leadership. . . . He represents all that is good about a leader. I'm a great believer in history, and I look at all the other leaders down through Yankee history, and Jeter is right there with them."

Don Mattingly

Donald Arthur Mattingly, affectionately known as "Donnie Baseball" to Yankee fans, was born in April 1961. He was selected by New York in the 1979 draft and made his Major League debut as a first baseman three years later. Though Mattingly never played on a World Series team with the Yankees, he was a six-time All-Star, a nine-time Gold Glove winner, and a three-time Silver Slugger. He was also named the 1985 AL MVP.

After Mattingly retired in 1995, his number was retired by the team. Two years later, he joined the Yankees as a special hitting instructor, and in 2003 he was named the team's hitting coach. In 2006, he was promoted to bench coach but left the team in 2007 after the departure of manager Joe Torre. He currently works alongside Torre with the Los Angeles Dodgers, and also runs Mattingly Sports, a baseball and softball equipment company founded in 2005.

Sure enough, Derek and the Yankees responded to the move. They won 20 out of 27 games during the month of June, earned 101 victories on the season, and finished 6 games ahead of their longtime rivals, the Boston Red Sox, in the American League East. Derek hit .324 with 87 runs scored and 52 RBIs in the regular season, and looked to continue his hot play during the playoffs.

BACK TO THE WORLD SERIES

New York defeated Minnesota in four games in the ALDS, setting up an American League Championship Series (ALCS) showdown against the Red Sox. The two teams had quite a history, and their playoff matchup in 2003 would add yet another chapter to the classic rivalry. The series was tied heading into game seven, which saw New York come back from a 4-0 **deficit** to win the game—and the series—in the 11th inning, thanks to a home run by Aaron Boone. The Yankees were heading back to the World Series.

The Florida Marlins provided the opposition in the 2003 World Series. The Yankees were heavy favorites coming into the series and took two of the first three games. However, the Marlins came back to take the next three to pull off the upset, becoming the second straight team to knock off New York in the World Series. Derek, who managed to hit .346 in the series

Derek throws out the Marlins' Luis Castillo in the first inning of game five of the 2003 World Series. After a nail-biting defeat of the Red Sox in the playoffs, the Yankees were favored to win the World Series. Their surprising loss to the Marlins saddened Derek, but he was determined that the team would come back strong the next season.

but was hitless in the sixth game, told reporters afterward that the loss made him feel "sick."

> **"They played better baseball than us. There's no sugarcoating it. They deserved to win."**

The Yankees weren't used to coming up short. Team owner George Steinbrenner certainly wasn't, manager Joe Torre wasn't, and neither was Derek. Though he began an on-again, off-again relationship with one-time Miss Teen USA and MTV personality Vanessa Minnillo during this time, it was obvious that he **yearned** to return to the baseball diamond and help the Yankees return to the form that had helped them win four World Series titles in five years.

GIVING IT ALL

Unfortunately for Derek, things were going to get worse before they got better. The shortstop struggled at the start of the 2004 season, enduring an 0-for-32 slump that was not only the worst of his career, but the worst by any Yankee player in 27 years. Rather than make excuses, though, Derek faced the adversity head-on and did whatever he could to overcome it, including working extra hours with New York hitting coach Don Mattingly. After all, as he told Ben Walker of the Associated Press,

> **"Pitchers aren't going to feel sorry for you. You've just got to go out and keep swinging."**

His approach worked. On April 29, he broke out of the slump with a home run against the Athletics. He hit .396 in the month of June. On July 1, during a game against the Red Sox, he drew attention for his defensive play. Derek dove headfirst into the stands to catch a fly ball and suffered facial injuries in the process. The play, which would become known as "The Dive," was voted the Play of the Year by MLB.com and showed exactly the lengths Derek would go to in order to help his team win.

In 2004 Derek led his team to the playoffs against the Boston Red Sox, whose intense rivalry with the Yankees has been delighting fans since 1901. It looked like the Yankees were sure to win, but the Sox came from behind to leave the Yankees in the dust on their way to the World Series.

Derek won his first career Gold Glove in 2004 and hit .292 with 23 home runs and 78 RBIs on the season—all while dating actresses Jessica Alba and Scarlett Johansson at times throughout the year. He was named the Player of the Week on September 13,

The 2005 season brought Derek new honors, including his first grand slam, a Gold Glove Award, and selection to play for Team USA in the World Baseball Classic, where he was named to the All-Tournament Team. His batting was also key in another Yankees trip to the playoffs.

hitting .436 with a pair of homers, 10 RBIs, and 11 runs scored during the week. He led New York back into the playoffs, setting up an ALCS rematch with Boston. This time, however, the Red Sox would get the better of the Bronx Bombers in a classic seven-game series.

Sports Rivalries: The Yankees and the Red Sox

Voted one of the 10 best rivalries in sports by ESPN, the New York Yankees versus the Boston Red Sox has long been one of the most intense matchups in Major League Baseball. The two teams first met in April 1901, when Boston was without an official team name and the Yankees franchise was still located in Baltimore. Three years later, Boston and New York first played for the American League pennant.

Since then, the New York Yankees and the Boston Red Sox have played more than 1,700 times, producing many memorable moments along the way. Babe Ruth was sold from Boston to New York, supposedly leading to a long-running series of post-season woes known as the "Curse of the Bambino." In 1978, New York's Bucky Dent hit a three-run homer to beat Boston in a one-game AL East playoff. In 2004, the Red Sox lost the first three games of the ALCS to the Yankees, only to come back and win in seven games en route to their first World Series title in 86 years.

NEW OPPORTUNITIES

In 2005, Derek appeared on the cover of the video game *MLB 2k5*. He batted .309 on the year while finishing second in the American League in runs scored with 122, and third in hits with 202. In June, he hit his first career grand slam, and he won his second straight Gold Glove Award as well. Once again, he helped the Yankees get to the playoffs, but they lost to the Angels in the first round. That December, Derek delivered toys to local children—an annual Christmas tradition of his, on behalf of his foundation.

Before the start of the Major League Baseball season, Derek was one of 30 players chosen to play for Team USA in the first World Baseball Classic. Although he told MLB.com it would feel strange playing for a team other than the Yankees, he also considered it an incredible honor.

> **"**I'm really excited to play for my country. I think it will be fun. I'm looking forward to it. It's going to be interesting. I've never had a chance to play for my country before.**"**

He made the most of the opportunity, hitting .450 and scoring five runs in six games during the Classic. Unfortunately, the United States went 3-3 and was eliminated in the second round. Japan went on to beat Cuba in the finals, and Derek was named to the All-Tournament Team for his outstanding play from the shortstop position.

World Baseball Classic

The World Baseball Classic (WBC) is a baseball tournament that pits teams from countries around the globe against each other. Originally announced in 2005, the WBC is the first worldwide baseball tournament to feature professional baseball players from Major League Baseball and other similar associations in other countries.

The first Classic was held in 2006 and featured 16 teams competing. In the semi-finals, Japan beat South Korea and Cuba knocked off the Dominican Republic, setting up a finals matchup between Japan and Cuba. The Japanese team won, 10-6, and also went on to win the 2009 WBC. The next WBC will be held in 2013 and will feature 24 international teams.

DRIVEN ON THE FIELD . . .

In August, 2006, Derek teamed with Avon to release a men's cologne called "Driven." However, "Driven" wasn't just the name of a product—it was the perfect way to describe the shortstop's play during the 2006 season. He finished second in the AL with a .343 batting average, posted a career-high 34 stolen bases, 118 runs scored, and 214 hits. He won both Gold Glove and Silver Slugger awards, and finished second in the MVP voting. He also collected his 2,000th career hit in May. However, as Derek told MLB.com, those individual honors and milestones were no big deal.

2000th HIT 2000
May 26, 2006

Derek snared his record 2,000th hit in a game against the Kansas City Royals on May 26, 2006. He also reached other milestones with Gold Glove and Silver Slugger awards. But Derek said he wasn't focusing on honors. He was more driven simply to help his team win.

" It's great, but we're trying to win games. Personal accolades you look at when your career is over with, or when the season is over with. Right now, I wasn't concerned about it. The bottom line is we're trying to win."

When it came to winning, Derek and the Yankees posted mixed results. New York won their ninth straight American League East division title. Once again, they made the playoffs, but

After the 2006 season, Derek focused on his charity work and held an annual golf event to benefit his Turn 2 Foundation. He was honored to accept an award from baseball legend Hank Aaron, who praised Derek for his many community efforts off the field.

just as in 2005, they failed to get out of the first round. This time, it was the Detroit Tigers who eliminated the Yankees in four games. Despite Derek's record-tying five-hit performance in game one, once again he and his teammates were denied a chance to compete for the World Series.

. . . AND OFF THE FIELD

Despite falling short of his ultimate goal of winning another World Series championship, he enjoyed one of the best years of his career. He posted a 25-game hitting streak during the year. Furthermore, in addition to his other honors, Derek was named the winner of the 2006 Hank Aaron Award for the most outstanding offensive performer in the American League. As Aaron said during the award presentation,

> **"Derek Jeter, to me, has demonstrated that he is not only a man that the Yankees can depend on winning a championship year in and year out, but he has carried this a little bit further because he has done so many great things off the field."**

True to form, Derek was once again involved in a number of off-the-field activities following the 2006 season. In November, he began dating actress Jessica Biel. A few months later, he was presented with the Oscar Charleston Award during a ceremony at the Negro League Hall of Fame. Early in 2007, he held his annual Celebrity Golf Classic, which raised money for the Turn 2 Foundation and the Derek Jeter Scholarship. Both on the field and off, he was quickly becoming the face of the New York Yankee franchise.

FACE OF
THE YANKEES

IN 2007, THE STAFF WRITERS AND READERS of ESPN.com named Derek Jeter the "Face of the Yankees." It's easy to see why he was selected for the honor. That season, he tallied more than 200 hits for the sixth time in his career, won the Silver Slugger award, and was voted into his eighth All-Star Game as well.

Looking back on his career, Derek was an obvious choice for the ESPN.com honor. His six 200-hits seasons were a Major League Baseball record for shortstops. When he was featured on the cover of *MLB 2k7*, it was the third time he had graced the front of the video game series. In fact, he was such a celebrity in 2007 that he was honored with a wax figure at Madame Tussauds in New York.

Derek's celebrity status was ensured in 2007 when he was named the "Face of the Yankees," after a record six 200-hit seasons. His famous batting stance was also captured in a wax figure unveiled at Madame Tussauds museum in New York.

PASSING THE YANKEE CLIPPER

On top of everything else, during the 2007 season Derek passed Yankee legend Joe DiMaggio on the team's all-time career hit list. He notched his 2,215th career hit during a May 24 game against the Boston Red Sox. Derek naturally downplayed the feat. Long-time manager Joe Torre, however, offered nothing but praise for the star player during an interview with MLB.com.

Celebrities in Wax

In 2007, Derek Jeter was added to a long list of celebrities who have been immortalized with a wax figure, either at Madame Tussauds or a similar wax museum. Entertainers such as *Hannah Montana* star Miley Cyrus, singer/actress Beyoncé, *American Idol* host Simon Cowell, and even the "King of Rock and Roll" himself, Elvis Presley, have their own figures at the Madame Tussauds New York location.

Furthermore, civil rights leader Martin Luther King, Jr. has been featured in wax. Madame Tussauds also has a statue dedicated to the first African-American President of the United States, Barack Obama, as well as former President Abraham Lincoln. Joining Derek in the sports wing are current players such as NBA basketball star Yao Ming and boxing great Muhammad Ali.

> "It's remarkable. . . . When you start putting those names up on the board, and i was here the whole time Derek was here, it's incredible. He's played 12 years, and every single year, he's been as consistent as you could ask for."

Torre wasn't the only one taking stock of Derek's remarkable accomplishments, however. Fans, sportscasters, and writers around the world had definitely taken notice. Mike Lupica, a longtime writer for the *New York Daily News*, reflected on Jeter's accomplishments during one of his columns. He summed up Derek's career beautifully:

> "He has been the DiMaggio of this Yankee era. . . . He does what he has always done, from the glory years until now: Shows up every day and plays hard. . . . Eventually he will play more games for the Yankees than anybody has ever played, honor the uniform as much as anybody who has ever worn it. . . . I asked him once how he sees himself, as a shortstop or a World Series champ or the captain of the team. 'I see myself as a Yankee,' Jeter said."

Derek leaps into the air to make an athletic play during a game against the Baltimore Orioles on September 28, 2007. Derek has been called the DiMaggio of the current Yankee era because he has consistently played hard and supported the team every year, just as the "Yankee Clipper" did in his day.

END OF AN ERA

New York qualified for the playoffs following the 2007 season, but once again they found themselves eliminated in the first round. For a team as rich in tradition as the Yankees, and for ownership as used to winning as the Steinbrenner family, such results were disappointing. In past years, whenever the team failed to win the American League pennant, the threat of massive changes to the team roster, the coaching staff, or the front office **loomed** large.

Following the 2007 season, the team parted ways with Joe Torre. Joe was the only manager Derek had played for as a Yankee, and definitely had a hand in shaping his career throughout the years. Upon learning of Torre's departure, Derek had this to say to Bryan Hoch of MLB.com:

Joe Torre, who managed the Yankees to four World Series victories, has been a huge influence on Derek's career. He has been Derek's friend and mentor, both on and off the field. When Torre left the Yankees after the 2007 season, Derek felt the loss deeply.

❝In my eyes, Joe Torre is more than a Hall of Fame manager. He is a friend for life, and the relationship we have shared has helped shape me in ways that transcend the game of baseball. . . . [T]here has been no bigger influence on my professional development. It was a privilege to play for him on the field, and an honor to learn from him off the field.❞

Joe Torre

Born on July 18, 1940, in Brooklyn, New York, Joe Torre was a professional baseball player for 18 seasons before becoming a manager. He was a nine-time All-Star, a former Gold Glove winner, and the 1971 National League MVP. Joe hit .297 on his career with 252 home runs and 1,185 RBIs. He started his managerial career with the New York Mets in 1977 but was never able to post a winning season. In 1982, he was named manager of the Atlanta Braves, where he won a division title in the first of his three years there.

After a stint as a broadcaster, Joe returned to managing in 1990 with the St. Louis Cardinals. He remained there until 1995, posting a 351-354 record with the team before being fired. From 1996 through 2007, he managed the Yankees to more than 1,100 wins and 4 World Series titles. Following his departure from the team, he took over as the manager of the Los Angeles Dodgers. In his first year with L.A. they won the National League West division title. It marked Joe's 13th straight playoff appearance as a manager.

Prior to the start of the 2008 season, Joe Girardi was hired to replace Torre as the Yankee manager. Girardi was named the 2006 National League Manager of the Year while with the Florida Marlins. Although the team had the lowest payroll in baseball that season, he turned Florida into playoff contenders. The hope heading into 2008 was that he could achieve even greater things managing a roster that included players such as Derek Jeter.

A BITTERSWEET SEASON

Unfortunately, things didn't exactly work out as planned. Girardi's first year as Yankee **skipper** got off to a rough start as the team went just 14-15 in April. In May, Derek was hit on the wrist by a pitch, and his play suffered as a result. By the end of the month, he was hitting just .262. Derek rebounded to make the All-Star Game once again. He also hit over .300 for the fourth consecutive year. As a team, though, the Yankees didn't fare as well, finishing with an 89-73 record and missing the playoffs.

During the season, Derek was named one of the "Gillette Champions" and began promoting the razor along with fellow athletic greats Roger Federer and Tiger Woods. He also filmed a Gatorade G2 commercial in 2008, further adding to a long list of endorsement deals that also included Visa, Ford, and XM Satellite Radio. He also hit his 400th career double and his 2,500th hit during the season, not to mention setting a new record for most hits at Yankee Stadium and moving into second place on the team's all-time hits list.

Personal achievements aside, the captain found it difficult to deal with the fact that his team had failed to qualify for the postseason for the first time in 13 years. Acting every bit the team captain and the "Face of the Yankees," Derek called the season a failure and set his sights on returning to the postseason the following year. Of course, he would be forced to endure a long off-season before he would have a chance at **redemption**.

CONTINUED HEROICS

In typical Derek Jeter fashion, however, he made the most of his time away from the game. For starters, he was named the captain of Team USA and participated in the 2009 World Baseball Classic. Also, prior to the start of the MLB season, Derek and David Wright of the New York Mets agreed to compete against each other for a good cause, with the player who posted the higher batting average earning his foundation $100,000 from Delta Air Lines.

On April 17, 2009, Derek hit a home run off Jensen Lewis of the Cleveland Indians, helping New York to their first-ever victory at new Yankee Stadium. As Girardi told MLB.com, Derek's heroics didn't exactly come as a surprise—he'd been doing it his entire career.

Derek throws to first for an out against the Boston Red Sox at Yankee Stadium on July 6, 2008. After rebounding from an injury in the 2008 season, Derek set a new record for hits at Yankee Stadium. Unfortunately he couldn't ensure that the Yankees would make the playoffs that year.

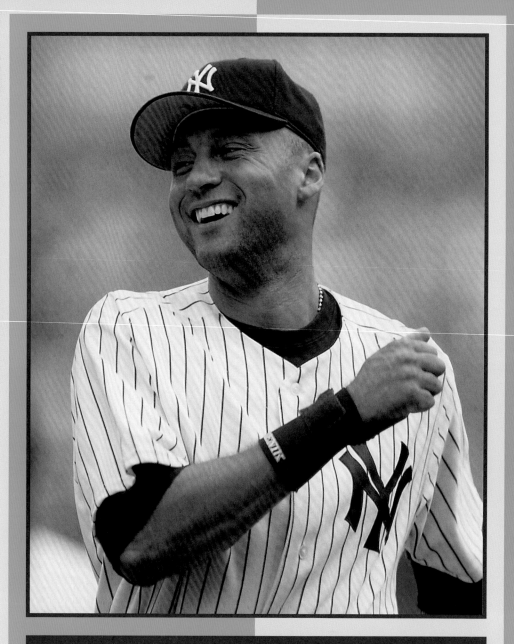

Derek's outstanding career has included four World Series championships and many awards for his offensive and defensive play. Derek enjoys these honors, but he continues to focus on the present, offering his unique skills to his team and his many fans, while building toward an already bright future.

"He's come up in a lot of big situations. . . . That's the type of player he's been his whole career. It's great. He's been a big part of this organization—Derek has been the face. It's a great job, and it's fitting."

A HALL OF FAME CAREER?

In his first 15 seasons with the Yankees, Derek Jeter has won four World Series championships, been honored for both his offensive and defensive play, and been to the All-Star game on many occasions. He is a career .300 hitter and has slowly but surely been breaking team records left and right. Furthermore, he has become a world-famous celebrity and has given much back to the community through his Turn 2 Foundation.

Odds are, his career is far from over. However, that hasn't kept both fans and sports media personalities, like MLB.com writer Bryan Hoch, from speculating about his chances of being inducted into the Baseball Hall of Fame. Hoch says,

"Jeter's reputation as a leader, clutch performer, and contributions for the Yankees' 1996–2000 World Series dynasty would readily outweigh any arguments [against]. . . . He has clearly been among the upper echelon of players in his era."

Time will tell whether or not Derek will join the likes of Babe Ruth, Lou Gehrig, Joe DiMaggio, Mickey Mantle, and the many other Yankee greats in the Hall of Fame. Judging by Derek's career, whatever the future holds, he will always give it his best effort.

1974 Derek Sanderson Jeter is born to Charles Jeter, an African American, and Dorothy Jeter, of Irish and German descent, on June 26 in Pequannock, New Jersey.

1978 The Jeter family moves to Kalamazoo, Michigan, so that Derek's father can earn a doctorate degree in psychology.

1989 Derek begins playing high school baseball as a freshman. He makes the varsity team at Kalamazoo Central High School.

1992 Derek is named the High School Player of the Year by the American Baseball Coaches Association, the Gatorade High School Athlete of the Year, and the *USA Today* High School Player of the Year.

He is drafted sixth overall by the New York Yankees in the 1992 Major League Baseball Draft. Derek is the first high-school player selected.

1993 In his first full season of minor league baseball, Derek is named Most Outstanding Major League Prospect by the managers of the South Atlantic League.

1994 Derek is named the Minor League Player of the Year by *USA Today*, *Baseball America*, and *The Sporting News*. He is also named the Most Valuable Player (MVP) of the Florida State League.

1995 On May 29, Derek makes his Major League debut. The following day, he collects his first career hit in the big leagues.

1996 Derek is named the starting shortstop on Opening Day, hits his first Major League home run, and is named the American League Rookie of the Year.

The Yankees win their first World Series since 1978; at the end of the year, Derek and his family start the Turn 2 Foundation.

1997 Derek receives votes for the AL MVP award for the first time after finishing third in the league with 191 hits.

1998 New York wins a team-record 114 games and their second World Series in three years. Derek finishes third in the MVP voting, is elected to the All-Star Game, and leads the AL in runs scored with 127.

1999 Derek sets career highs in several statistical categories, including batting average, home runs, and RBIs, to help the Yankees to a second-straight World Series championship.

2000 Derek becomes the first person in baseball history to win All-Star Game and World Series MVP awards in the same season. His efforts help New York win a third straight World Series title.

2001 Derek hits his first All-Star Game home run, and the Yankees once again win the American League pennant. However, they fall to the Arizona Diamondbacks in the World Series.

2002 Derek becomes the fourth player in Major League Baseball history to score 100 runs or more during each of his first seven professional seasons.

2003 Derek is named captain of the New York Yankees.

2004 For the first time in his career, Derek's defensive play is recognized as he wins a Gold Glove Award. He helps the Yankees win 101 games and reach the playoffs for the 10th consecutive season.

2005 Derek finishes second in the American League with 122 runs scored and third with 202 hits. New York wins the American League East.

2006 Derek participates in the first-ever World Baseball Classic. He also finishes second in the voting for the AL MVP, wins his first Silver Slugger Award, and helps New York to their ninth straight division title.

2007 Derek is named the "Face of the Yankees" by ESPN.com. He sets a Major League Baseball record with his sixth 200-hit season and is named to the AL All-Star Team for the eighth time.

2008 Derek reaches several personal milestones. He gets his 2,500th career hit in August, passes Babe Ruth for second on the Yankees' all-time hits list, and breaks Lou Gehrig's record for most career hits at Yankee Stadium.

2009 On April 17, Derek hits a home run to give New York their first victory at their new ballpark, also named Yankee Stadium.

Awards

1992   ABCA High School Player of the Year
Gatorade High School Athlete of the Year
USA Today High School Player of the Year

1993   Most Outstanding Major League Prospect, South Atlantic League

1994   *USA Today* Minor League Player of the Year
Baseball America Minor League Player of the Year
The Sporting News Minor League Player of the Year
Florida State League Most Valuable Player

1996   American League Rookie of the Year

1998   All-Star Game player

1999   All-Star Game player

2000   All-Star Game Most Valuable Player
World Series Most Valuable Player

2001   All-Star Game player

2002   All-Star Game player

2004   All-Star Game player
Gold Glove Award

2005   Gold Glove Award

2006   All-Star Game player
Gold Glove Award
Hank Aaron Award
Silver Slugger Award

2007   Named "Face of the Yankees" by ESPN.com
All-Star Game player
Silver Slugger Award

2008   All-Star Game player
Silver Slugger Award

Championships

1996   World Series Champion with New York Yankees

1998   World Series Champion with New York Yankees

1999   World Series Champion with New York Yankees

2000   World Series Champion with New York Yankees

Career Statistics (through April 23, 2009)

Games	2,000
At-Bats	8,088
Runs	1,476
Hits	2,553
Doubles	414
Triples	57
Home Runs	210
RBIs	1,012
Walks	818
Strikeouts	1,384
Stolen Bases	277
Batting Average	.316

Big Apple—another name for New York City.

deficit—in baseball, the number of runs one team is behind another.

hiatus—time off; a period of time spent away from a certain activity.

inauspicious—not as successful as one had hoped.

irate—very angry.

loomed—hung over in a threatening way.

milestones—important achievements.

persevered—worked hard to overcome problems.

prowess—talent or ability.

redemption—the act of restoring the reputation of someone or something.

skipper—baseball slang for a manager.

unanimously—without any objection; in the case of awards, receiving 100% of the vote.

venerable—old and respected.

yearned—wanted very badly; longed for.

Books

Christopher, Matt. *On the Field with . . . Derek Jeter*. New York: Little, Brown Young Readers, 2000.

Giles, Patrick. *Derek Jeter: Pride of the Yankees*. New York: St. Martin's Press, 1999.

Jeter, Derek. *Game Day: My Life on and off the Field*. New York: Three Rivers Press, 2001.

Jeter, Derek. *The Life You Imagine: Life Lessons for Achieving Your Dreams*. New York: Three Rivers Press, 2001.

Marcovitz, Hal. *Derek Jeter*. Broomall, Pennsylvania: Mason Crest Publishers, 2008.

Web Sites

http://derekjeter.mlb.com/players/jeter_derek/index.jsp

This is the official online home of the Yankee shortstop, loaded with information and exciting features about his life and career. Catch up on the latest Derek Jeter news, then check out the trivia section to test your baseball I.Q. There are also photo galleries, digital downloads, and highlights of great plays dating back to 2004.

http://www.mlb.com/players/jeter_derek/turn2/index.jsp

The homepage for Derek's Turn 2 Foundation is hosted on his official Web site. Here, you can find out all about his charitable foundation, including events, the group's mission statement, and more. It's a cool way to keep up-to-date on how the Yankee captain is giving back to the community and making a difference in the lives of kids all over the world.

http://newyork.yankees.mlb.com/index.jsp?c_id=nyy

Of course, no online tour of Derek Jeter–themed Web sites would be complete without a stop at the official page of his team, the New York Yankees. Here you can keep tabs on the team, check out recent and upcoming games, find out when they'll be on TV, order tickets, and much more. There's even a ton of info on Yankee Stadium, video highlights, downloadable schedule, and stuff for your mobile phone.

PICTURE CREDITS

ABOUT THE AUTHOR

Chuck Bednar is an author and freelance writer from Ohio. He has been writing professionally since 1997 and has written more than 1,500 published nonfiction articles. Bednar is also the author of eight books, including the *Tony Parker* and *Tim Duncan* entries in Mason Crest's MODERN ROLE MODELS series, as well as SUPERSTARS OF PRO FOOTBALL: *Tony Romo*. He is currently employed by Bright Hub (www.brighthub.com) as the Managing Editor for their Nintendo Wii Web site.